The Mother's Milk Books Writing Prize Anthology 2015

LOVE

Also by Teika Bellamy

Editor:

Musings on Mothering (Mother's Milk Books 2012)

Letting Go by Angela Topping (Mother's Milk Books 2013)

Look At All The Women by Cathy Bryant (Mother's Milk Books 2014)

The Mother's Milk Books Writing Prize Anthology 2013: PARENTING (Mother's Milk Books 2014)

The Forgotten and the Fantastical (Mother's Milk Books 2015)

Hearth by Sarah James and Angela Topping (Mother's Milk Books 2015)

Oy Yew by Ana Salote (Mother's Milk Books 2015)

The Mother's Milk Books Writing Prize Anthology 2014: THE STORY OF US (Mother's Milk Books 2015)

Echolocation by Becky Cherriman (Mother's Milk Books 2016)

The Forgotten and the Fantastical 2 (Mother's Milk Books 2016)

Maysun and the Wingfish by Alison Lock (Mother's Milk Books 2016)

Handfast by Ruth Aylett and Beth McDonough (Mother's Milk Books 2016)

Baby X by Rebecca Ann Smith (Mother's Milk Books 2016)

The Mother's Milk Books Writing Prize
Anthology 2015

LOVE

Edited by Teika Bellamy

Mother's Milk Books

First published in Great Britain in 2016 by Mother's Milk Books

Front cover image 'Untitled' copyright © Lois Rowlands 2008
Cover design copyright © Teika Bellamy 2016
Foreword copyright © Teika Bellamy 2016
Poetry judge's report copyright © Sarah James 2016
Prose judge's report copyright © Zion Lights 2016

ISBN 978-0-9954516-3-6

Typeset in Georgia and Aaargh by Teika Bellamy.
Aaargh font designed by Tup Wanders.
Printed and bound in Great Britain by The Russell Press, Nottingham,
on FSC paper and board sourced from sustainable forests.
www.russellpress.com

First published in 2016 by Mother's Milk Books
www.mothersmilkbooks.com

SPECIAL THANKS TO:

Sarah James and Zion Lights
for their considered and thoughtful judging.
Saffia Farr at *JUNO* magazine for her generosity
in donating prizes of back issues of *JUNO* magazines
and for first publishing the winning entries
in the Summer 2016 issue of *JUNO* (issue 44).

CONTENTS

Foreword

Back in autumn 2015, when the third Mother's Milk Books Writing Prize was open to submisions, I couldn't wait to see what would be sent our way. Once again, the annual prize received a bumper crop of wonderful submissions. Both the judges, Sarah James and Zion Lights were impressed by the high standard of entries and we were all happily surprised by the ways in which the writers interpreted the theme 'Love', in a family context.

This year I also got to choose some of my own favourite prose and poetry pieces; I knew I simply had to publish these pieces in this anthology and so awarded them with the commendation of 'Publisher's Choice'.

I am, as ever, very grateful to all the writers who sent in their work and I hope that the prize will continue to receive excellent writing for many years to come.

Enjoy!

Teika Bellamy, Autumn 2016

Poetry Judge's Report

Reading the entries to this competition was a delight. Family love covered grandparents, new parents and wider family. There was thought, imagination and feeling – love – in every poem. Sometimes I was close to crying, other times I could feel myself smiling.

Choosing between these poems was the hard part. I read and re-read the entries several times on different days in different places, in my head and aloud. Writing up my report, I fell more and more in love with the anthology poems as my admiration for them grew: their structure, line breaks, imagery and more. Many of the poems that weren't commended also had some beautiful lines and haunting images contained within them.

The Adult Category

WINNER:
It was a close call, but in the end 'Janet' was the piece that stayed with me most each time. It is a beautifully spare poem, in which every word (and punctuation mark) earns its keep. I tested my own judgement. I asked myself could it hold its place against the rich lines of some of the other poems. Every time I doubted it, it answered back with an insistent yes. In just ten lines, this poem manages the feat of both being about a very specific moment – a new mum going to comfort her child at night – and the whole of two women's lives as "all the women we'll become | gather silently around us." The focus is tight, precise and controlled. One haunting image is the moon "scuffed | and thin and over-bright." I can imagine in a workshop, someone might query an object being both "scuffed"

and "overbright". Yet, not only can I see a bright moon that is scuffed in places by mist, I can also see new motherhood shining through – a mother's face over-bright with joy, scuffed around the edges by tiredness. A lovely poem that wins through with its wonderfully measured quiet confidence.

COMMENDEDS:

'I Measure My Mother's Love' is a vivid, evocative poem that captures the mother's love through her sewing. Beautifully structured, this moves through the threads, buttons and fabrics the mother used, each also evoking the person that the clothes belong to. But love is not just in the choice of materials, it is also in the actual making "In rustless needles and blood-sharp pins, | in running stitches tacking shapeless fabric | to lithesome bodies and coltish limbs." It is also in the way that love adapts, captured wonderfully in the closing lines: "in turned down hems, let down as we grew."

'Us' is a poem about ten years of marriage and "what lies hidden in our ordinary love." It moves wonderfully from the outward reality of "our damp house, near the city, | where my uncertain self, talks us | from everywhere to somewhere" to what lies behind this: "Did you know, our suburb was a waterland." With this line, the poem really takes off at both a literal and metaphorical level. As I read, I imagine a typical estate home that literally has been built on reclaimed floodland. Metaphorically, this analogy picks up on so much of what is extraordinary about "ordinary love."

'Music' is another wonderfully spare poem that captures new motherhood: "Sometimes in the night | I forget you." This is not a real forgetting though, more a merged existence, felt all the more in the tiredness at night when "our boundaries are as blurred | as yesterday's dreams." This poem took me straight back to when my own children were babies.

'Poem for Imogen' is another poem that not only allows spare lines to carry its emotional weight but deepens that emotional impact by doing so. It also uses sewing/knitting both literally and symbolically, culminating in a wonderful final line for a very moving poem about losing a baby: "A dropped stitch in time".

'Josef' is another very moving poem, where simple, spare and controlled lines and images enhance the emotional thrust. They also add extra strength to those few places were richer imagery is used, such as: "your neck is a daisy stem | your uncurled hand a starfish | beached." There is so much that I admire in this poem, including the line breaks, evocative use of all the senses and a striking concluding couplet.

'Volume' is one of the few poems that manages the lovely feat of balancing both the joy and sadness of being a parent. Each line flows naturally from the previous, with the layout giving the words both space to breathe and space to grow into – rather as the unnamed child/children do in the poem until "the living room is full of legs." It also neatly captures both aspects of volume: space and sound.

'Valentine's Day' is very different to many of the poems that I read for the competition, and the one that really pulled off being different, right from the bold opening line and stanza: "Valentine's Day was liver coloured... wet with deceit and drama." At this point, I was maybe expecting a poem about the sham of February 14th and romance compared to real love. But there is far more than that to the poem, as the contrast is revealed to be to an 11-year-old daughter's love, reacting to the loss of her father. This is a gripping and moving poem, full of drama – a drama that justifies itself because it is an 11-year-old's viewpoint.

'Their house is a slipper' is a poem that is every bit as warm as its opening lines suggest: "Their house is a slipper, I step inside | and it brings the comfort of a cup of tea." Not only is a slipper comfortable, but it made me think of the nursery rhyme of the old woman who lived in a shoe. And what we have in this house is a nan who fills it with stories, smiles and laughter. I very much felt as a reader that I was not only in this house beside the narrator, with the poem's wonderfully real and specific details, but very much welcomed there as part of the family. I left the poem, as I suspect the narrator does the house, with a warm glow.

'Springsong' is a poem that I wanted to share because of its combination of accessible, simple images with a non-conventional use of language (merging words) and layout. I left this poem with a smile on my face and song inside me, as it confidently delivers the promise of its title.

'Water Baby' is again a poem that very much lives up to its title. It's not unusual to find water and sea imagery connected to pregnancy and birth, and this fact makes it an all the more striking feat when such a framework is used successfully. The 'baby swimmer' metaphor is sustained without being over-egged from first to last line of this poem, and particularly strongly in the third stanza where "You came eagerly, | running the bow wave."

'The Laughing Day, the Hours of Breathing' is a poem of opening out to the world, and as such manages to create a very full picture. The core of this poem is the narrator's dying father. But it opens with the sound of children laughing somewhere else inside or near to the hospital and "the only time | of life when screams signify fun." In doing so, the poem not only captures a very personal grief but also the place of that grief within the wider world. This contrast is sustained throughout the poem, where we later see nature in full beauty outside, making the loss unfolding within that hospital even more moving. There is some beautiful imagery in the poem too, from "His lungs were an orchestra tuning up, | his flickering tongue conducting | the bass rasps and grunts of effort" to "My father's beard should be blossoms | or feathers, not snow. It moves to the clumsy, | clunky clockwork of lung-time."

The Children's Category

Judging this competition really made me think hard about the various elements that make for a good poem and how to prioritise them. There is, of course, no one recipe for success. Choosing between these poems was a difficult, and ultimately subjective, task, particularly when all the entries seemed full of very real love, thought and crafting. There were also some excellent attempts at rhyme and using repetitive structures.

In the end, I chose 'An Austin Morning' as my winner. This poem is perhaps closer to prose than many of the other entries. But it holds its own rhythm and creates a very clear picture of what is announced in the title. The poem uses the sense of sound, as well as sight, to make the scene come alive. It also makes good use of strong verbs, metaphors and similes. The end lines bring a very confident close to the poem.

COMMENDEDS:
'Why I write poetry (To Dad)' – I found it impossible not to feel full of light and love reading this simple but heartfelt poem with its compelling rhythm and end-line rhymes.

'Get Along' is a poem that I admired for its different take on the theme of family love, focussing on sibling love/arguing and then widening it to explore what family actually means, with two confident final lines.

'Sisters' also takes a sibling relationship as its subject, but this time its strength is in keeping that focus tight, precise and filled with emotion.

'Lanora's love poem' – this is a delightful poem to read: simple, beautiful, genuine, with a lovely opening out to the reader/audience in the final line.

'Forever Love' – this quietly confident poem makes great use of repetition and the list form to illustrate and gradually expand what family love is.

Sarah James, Spring 2016

Prose Judge's Report

Sometimes the weeks fly by but the days are long. This is how I was feeling when I sat down with the prose entries for this writing prize, ready to immerse myself in the written worlds of the mothers who had contributed their stories, and wash away some of the day's tribulations by doing so. What I found surpassed my expectations, as I went on one mother's journey to another's, their tales as varied and textured as our individual parenting journeys naturally are. Sometimes we need fresh eyes to be reminded of the beautiful moments of motherhood, and also to remember that the difficult moments will pass. I felt energised by these writing entries, and set the unread stories aside, to be approached another day with fresh eyes, and with a heart that would feel less raw to the lens of the beautiful but turbulent journey that is parenting. Then I travelled the textured road again, and was blown away by its wonders.

WINNER:
'Nurturing My Darkness' – It's rare to read a piece of writing that touches on what one feels as a parent in this world, that connects you with the rest of humanity and makes you feel less alone. For me, 'Nurturing My Darkness' did exactly this. "Take your time and breathe, mama." it begins. "It's okay." Instantly I took a breath. I read a lot of non-fiction for my work and the open and direct, raw emotional style of this writing spoke to me in a deep way. It made me feel less alone, as I became lost and then immersed in the words this writer was offering me, those of consolation and of understanding, I wept a mother's tears at the end. To the author I send a heartfelt thank you for this work of prose, for writing the words that every mother sometimes needs to hear on those dark days.

COMMENDEDS:

'My Gadabout Gran' – I never had grandparents, never knew them at all. This work paints a touching and nostalgic picture of the writer's grandmother, much as I would have expected my own to be. Gran likes to travel. Gran is like a butterfly. Gran becomes a memory, captured by the writer in a wonderful vignette.

'The Lens of Love' – This is another raw and open emotional piece that, for me, captures the love of a mother in a very unique way. This mother feels what I feel and have felt on my parenting journey, and also captures the utterly sacrificial nature of a mother's love. The delicate writing style is especially captivating in this piece.

'The Swing' – When does one become a mother? Reading this work, I felt that it happens long before the baby arrives. This mother craves her unborn baby, imagines in detail the child she longs to have but has not yet been able to conceive. I understand her longing and her need, as do so many women around the world. This writer brings those childless mothers together with her story.

'Anything Could Happen' – With a parent's love also comes the difficulties – the side we don't like to talk about, as this writer admits about her child: "I desperately want to like her more." This work is bold and brave, just as this mother is fiercely determined to make the best of an incredibly difficult situation. I bow my head to her.

'The Spinning' – The love before children. The love of two adults caught in the magical world of each other. Then children, family, and loss. This story made me spin with its many stories, meshed and unravelling together, as families do. Wonderful storytelling.

'I Am Ready' is a light and positive musing on a mother's readiness for her baby and child, for the journey we take together when we become mothers and are mothered. This honest and open work provides a refreshing read.

'The Miracle of Love' will take you on a rollercoaster journey of grief, loss and love. I haven't experienced this type of loss myself but of course we will all go through it some time – parental loss is very real and also very much something that we don't talk about. I appreciate the frank tone of this work, and the sharing of the story.

'Mother's Day' tells a similar tale of mourning and yearning, but in a different way. There is loss and sadness, but also acceptance. I felt that a powerful process was tackled by this powerful work of prose.

'Love Is...' paints a wonderful picture of everyday parenting moments that we don't always get the chance to savour. I enjoyed reliving some surprisingly similar moments through this work, and the warm idea of my child "curled up against [my future] middle aged spread."

Zion Lights, Spring 2016

Publisher's Choice

The Adult Poetry Category

'Now' gives a precise and not-overly sentimental "showing" of a grandmother's love for her grandson. I think it paints the scene with skill and care, and I am touched by the love in it.

'First Night Away' is a spare poem, but which conjures the sense of what it is like to have an older child go away for a night very well. I love the phrase: "All night creaks of him;" which sums up what it's like to be a parent, anxious and disquieted by the sounds of the night while thinking of their child.

'Belly' is simply very different to the rest, and refreshingly so. It makes me smile and I love the last two lines (which I won't give away here). I like the way it is about the unconditional love that a child has for us, and how this is non-judgemental and how they can help us to see (what we consider) our flaws as something altogether different, and positive.

'Owen Learning' is on the theme of breastfeeding, and I think the fact that it is from the grandmother's perspective interesting. It contains some lovely images of the baby after he has fed: "the sated smile, bloated belly | of a little king;".

'My Turn' is a successful poem which conjures up the scene of an elderly father struggling in the night very well. I love some of the imagery and the last line is understated yet powerful.

With the poem, 'Baby' I simply adore some of the imagery — the "white cloths" (terry towel nappies) as "clouds of butterflies" particularly resonated with me.

The Adult Prose Category

'What Will Survive of Us is Love' is a beautifully poetic paean to the life of a long-term couple with young children and I was glad to see the author celebrating the everyday joys of what many think of as a stagnant time in a couple's life.

Although our family don't home educate, the piece 'Love and Home Education' spoke to me as, ultimately, the piece is about making decisions that are hard because close family members disagree with our choices. It's about standing strong, making those decisions anyway, and having the grace to accept that others may think differently, and that that's okay.

'Love Ain't Enough' expresses the notion that the word 'love' is very much over-used today. And yet, our love for our children can be very strong. What the author is looking for is a "love PR guru" – which I very much like the idea of!

'Ashes' is a gentle and beautiful recounting of the loss of a grandmother and the scattering of her ashes. It is well-written and powerful in an understated way, and reminds me of the importance of family at the end of one's life, at the ultimate transformative experience, death.

I am delighted to be able to publish all the above pieces within the anthology and only wish we had room for more!

Teika Bellamy, Spring 2016

Us

We married in summer, in lion-long days,
ten years ago, and I have loved you
deeply, from before that day, to this.
We have imagined each other,
the soul of our marriage,
in this, our damp house, near the city,
where my uncertain self, talks us
from everywhere to somewhere.
At night, we settle down,
our feet pointing west over the streetlights.
Did you know, our suburb was a waterland;
our roof a home for waterbirds,
our door a reedbed, our faces, edged
in flow, sprung from the black earth's depths
where creatures, long extinct, have swum?
This is what lies hidden in our ordinary love,
a watery man and woman, silhouetted
by a dateless moon, paired for life, legendary;
safe; rilling their course together.

ALISON JONES

The Swing

'What's your greatest fear, Miss?' one of my pupils asks me, as she finds her place in the front row and settles into her seat.

Surprised, I continue to look at my monitor.

She tries again: 'Miss, what is your worst fear?'

'That's a very personal question,' I say. I know what my worst fear is; it gnaws away at me every day. But I can't tell her that; say it out loud. 'I fear that I won't be able to achieve everything that I want to in this life.'

My response wasn't what she was expecting. For a moment, her gaze and tongue still.

'I'm afraid of snakes.'

'Oh, I'm not afraid of creatures,' I say.

Our bond broken, she turns to her friends and directs her question to them; I prepare to quieten the class and start the lesson.

Perhaps it's time to admit it to myself. If I can't say it, then I must write it. I can't imagine life without children of my own: this is my worst fear. I'm left breathless at the thought. So I'll imagine my child; bring her to life in my imagination so I will believe in her and have faith in the future. Remain hopeful.

Of course, this is easier said than done.

Everyone tells me to stay positive: 'I know someone with polycystic ovaries who has had children.'

'Don't Posh Spice and Jools Oliver have that? And they have four children each!'

*

I know this; yet something inside me gives way every time I hear it, like losing your footing whilst climbing or pulling the piece in Jenga that makes the whole tower tumble down, piece by piece.

I must stay positive but my Facebook Newsfeed insistently fills with comments of friends' joyful news: more babies, scans, status updates, another brother or sister for little Millie or Jack. The pain of it.

Having always taken pleasure in such joyful news, I am taken aback by the jolt of pain, quickly followed by stabbing guilt at this negative, envious emotion. Announcements of a second child conceived, unlocks the questions: why? How is it fair that they can seemingly – so easily – have another child when I am struggling to conceive my first?

A good friend of mine recently called me to say that she is pregnant for the second time. Did my congratulations sound forced?

'No one is as interested the second time you get pregnant. When is your husband going to let you have children?'

There hadn't been an opportunity to tell her in person that we had decided we wanted to start a family and that I had come off the pill a year ago. I paused. Now wasn't the right time either.

'Will he let you before you're 40?'

I managed to laugh. We're in our early thirties; there's still time.

'We'll have to see.'

So, longed for child of my imagination, I commit you to the page now – my beloved – stay with me now and always.

Dark like night your hair; unruly like mine. *Bhisri* your Dad calls it. Your face lit up by an impish glint in your eyes. Playfully you run ahead to the swing not yet hung on the tree branch not yet grown. You are old enough to no longer need a push but you still insist that we do. I'm reluctant to push you too hard, but your Dad shares the same impish glint in his eyes

25

as you and I watch as you soar higher and higher, into the heavens.

God-willing, from heaven you'll fall.

RACHEL PATEL

Volume

you were never nothing

though I can't trace the line
of matter back

you were simply other
then you made yourself

the trick of clotting cell soup
into ravelled flesh is automatic

and I let you run
fill the space   crescendo

now you are tall
and the living room is full of legs

the house bursting with stuff
stuck to the edges of your life

when you go
there'll be a cavern

echoes

JAN DEAN

First Night Away

All night creaks of him; half-dreams shush
strange swirlaround sighs. Calls
crack sored air as breaths
draught under doors, curtains
stir. Toast scratches deep
inside his burrowed
pillow smells. We tense,
alert to pace till dawn eyes
printout that cold
empty bed next door.

BETH MCDONOUGH

The Spinning

You meet.

And every meeting is different.

Bloody Disney. You grow up thinking that each party might deliver a prince, that your eyes will meet and your heart will know. But these are profitable human constructions. Nature, in its raw and experimental chemistry, has other ideas.

A Story: University. There's been... something. Flirting? Not quite that. Your mutual friend is in a teasing mood.

'So would you?'

'I don't know what you mean.'

'Yes you do. If he asked you.'

I answer with all the certainty of someone who knows things only from books.

'Not if he was the last man on earth.'

At a point between falling in lust and falling in love your hands enfold fiercely like the legs of displaced spiders, clasping strong one to another and the silken thread begins to entwine, unseen, but tangible to both of you. Magic. May he always be yours and you his and before you know it, you're dancing in silk, in a web of your making, sticky, sparkling, turning raindrops to jewels and bending in the wind.

But nature's having a joke surely? You argue, but not in the same way. Who does that? Who follows those 'how to argue positively' guidelines, beloved of Sunday supplements? No, no: there must be lustful shouting. Your threads feel beautiful webbed together, but my, the tensile strengths are different. You're not similar at all. You're not even similar enough to be opposites. You have nothing in common except that you find in each other your mate and you laugh every day. And then at some point it dawns that neither of you will leave, ever, that no one is walking – or, about to change significantly for that matter – and that there's no danger in honesty, because... really? *Really?*

Turns out the last man on earth is a keeper.

A Story: It's raining. I'm standing elbow deep in bubbles, watching the drops bounce off the hazel, smiling at the tot walking down the road with her too big umbrella and for no particular reason, I think of him. I wonder what he's doing.

I dry my hands and reach for my phone and before I touch Messages, the phone vibrates and he's there, in my inbox. Webs span gaps too great for crawling. It's like he heard my thoughts, my tap on the ties. Hi. How is your morning going? The rain falls. The child in the street laughs. So this is family.

Summer. You wear baby blue shoes, your new married name scrawled in marker pen on your knickers, a sparkling love heart on your back and you begin immediately to make your family bigger. Nature's chemistry works. The threads may not line up perfectly (your web is distinctly unsymmetrical) but your happiness makes beautiful babies. She's born with the wind, angry, blue, wild.

And no one tells you, do they? That along with the gifts of bootees and blankets and a hundred things you discover you really don't need, there's a spinning.

Does it happen in that first night, when you sleep for thirty seconds at a time, your babe beside you, pale as a pupa, not quite of this world? Perhaps they glide unseen, those invisible threads, in those still few seconds and twine quietly under her skin, while hers, thin and light as gossamer, tumble round your heart and hold it tight. You are bound, the cord replaced by invisible silks that hum and sing, cranking into communication and pulsing strongly.

A Story: My baby had stopped moving. Alone, quietly worried, I spoke to her. 'Are you okay?' An immediate kick back and I'm smitten.

After she's born I'm so exhausted I cry every other day, just by way of punctuation. But broken though my body feels, I wake a minute before her cry, somehow receiving warning of her need, so that when the whimper comes, my arms are ready. Not much makes any impact on my sleep-deprived mind, but this telepathy feels like a reward. I'm doing something right. How can I argue with magic? I'll keep going.

Those early months I looked around our cottage and wondered where my life had gone. Books unread, newspapers piled, hair uncut, a drifting experience in a sleepless bubble. There were many times I stepped outside and my eyes went into distance shock, having focussed only on what was in my arms for days at a time. We do a disservice to those who come behind us to pretend that the tough side of family love doesn't exist. Even though I'd barely have listened, I wish someone had taken me aside, fed me cake and said, 'There's some stuff – some crappy stuff – that you should know. And it happens to us all.'

We manage though don't we, us mothers? Our days are filled with snot or smiles, our floors are sticky and our wardrobes limited, but not one of us would have things as they were before we became a mother. We're jelly and tough and forever.

(Story: A dark one. I'll hide it here. Small.)
Not always though. Not every mother.

31

'I don't know why I even had you.'

It's tossed carelessly, as others are. It takes time to undo the web, to get out uneaten, but I gather to me what's frayed and move on.

We have another tiny girl and then twins. Do I need to say that my house is noisy and messy? That there was utter joy as each new sibling became entwined with the others? Their bonds are fierce, independent of us, and they are always together, reading, dancing, imagining, laughing. Life is bigger than it has ever been. I get more sleep, but answer more questions and these threads round my heart, pulse all day, sensitive – if I let them – to who's feeling happy and who needs a hug. A mama's radar is a powerful instrument. Dad's too.

When spiders need to leave they throw themselves into the wind and wait for their silk to find something to adhere to. Many are blown huge distances. Nature allows for such miracles and some land on ships far out to sea, puzzling the sailors who find them far beyond land. The tensile strength of spider silk is greater than that of steel. There is no need to assume that nature has furnished your mind and heart with anything less incredible.

An End(ing) story: On this particular Sunday he was still in the normal ward. He was poorly, frail, grey and gummy eyed, but not yet hooked to the machines that would breathe hideously for him in those final weeks. His face warmed when he saw her.

'I love you Papa,' she lisped, a two-year-old puzzled that he didn't pick her up today.

'I love you too darling.'

Before he died I asked him if he remembered that she'd been to see him. Loss in his eyes. Confusion. Anger at himself. 'No. I don't remember.'

Years later I asked if she remembered the meeting. Or her Papa at all.

'No... No I don't remember.'

But I was there. I saw their thread, humming with love, quietly ignoring flesh and time.

LYNN BLAIR

Springsong

chorus
outside
as blackbirds
sing the sun
     –   the first
       Springsong
       we have
          together
             shared.
our muted gaze
liftsandlocks
across your sleeping form
     –   pearlcurled
          between us
our lips-sync in smile
and you stir
     –   deepsleepblush
       to morningburst
as your joyful voice
greets
the day
in chorus.

CATHERINE SMITH

Baby

The armful of baby warms me. There are white cloths
in their thousands like clouds of butterflies.
The washing machine gives endless droning speeches.

Wiping, washing, washing, wiping. Sudden smiles,
laughter. Struggles to help the tiny person convey
what he is trying to say, jerking his disobedient limbs
and head. He screams in frustration. Like being
in prison, being a baby. It is my job to lead you out.

Your first word attempts are as precious as platinum:
buh – wuh – ah – bah – ma – wah. Frustrated again,
this time by my failure to understand. Oh little one,
my dear love, you are too young to have learned
the joy of patience, the pleasure in waiting as, drop
by drop, the grape juice becomes champagne.

The gifts you give! Trust, as you relax flopped on
my stomach. Your explosions of helpless laughter.
Snatches of sleep bring the cloths and clothes again,
piled up in dreams, washed again, dried again, then
wrapping the incredible child so we can take wing.

CATHY BRYANT

I Am Ready

I sit staring at this precious bundle in front of me, his head nuzzled into my chest. An honour. Just two weeks since my body opened to make way for his epic journey from the comfort and safety of my womb to the openness and fragility of my arms. He wanted to be with us; he was ready to be with us; so he came. He came. He is here. He really is here. My baby, my son, my prince of peace, one day to be a King... but for now I cradle this majestic little soul in my arms, listening intently to his tiny murmurings and the gentle rhythm of his heart; feeling his soft warm skin awakening the aliveness of my body; breathing in the milky scent of his newness... this is pure pleasure... surely THIS is Love.

It seems that just as the bones of my pelvis parted to allow for his arrival into the world, so too did the gates of my heart. He came calling with the gentle knocking of a soul in search of Love... and I answered... my heart peeled wide open, allowing a free-flow of Love to pour, cleansing my soul as do the tears that flow tenderly from my eyes; nourishing my baby as does the milk that flows freely from my breasts; healing my body as does the blood that flows gracefully from the closing of my womb. Is this what Love feels like? It is a funny feeling; I find it kind of strange to feel so open, so absorbed in this sacred bubble of Love that engulfs me and the beautiful treasure in my arms. Yet somehow it is a familiar place, like coming home, for there is no doubt that it is cradled in the arms of Love that we all belong. This is Love. This is Home.

But how is it that this place I call 'home' is a place I have visited so infrequently? How is it that these feelings of pure Love seem so new when I know deep down they are my birthright? How is it that I haven't allowed myself to open up to this feeling since I was just a little girl myself, eyes bright, staring in wonder at the world around me?

Somehow it hurts. I'm afraid, afraid of the vulnerability, afraid of what it means to expose my heart in this way, afraid of what might happen, what wounding might be inflicted on this oh-so-precious part of me. And then I remember, 'Grace has brought me safe thus far and Grace will lead me home'. But actually, I'm already there. I've arrived. I'm safe. I'm home. I'm here, I'm ready, I'm opening once more to Love.

For sure, I've tried my best to resist. After all, this little angel that is opening my heart in such a way is the third child that has passed through my body and danced into life with me to call its mother. For five years of motherhood, I've managed to keep myself closed, my heart guarded fiercely by brave soldiers, fighting to protect me from such searing pain as once was felt. For five years, I've mothered two other children, cared for them, nursed them, slept beside them, offered them empathy, support and closeness. I've whispered 'I love you' to them a thousand times over, but I never truly meant it because my heart wasn't truly open to receiving them. I desperately wanted to – but I couldn't – not until now.

What a beautiful gift their brother has brought to them – finally, they have a mother who is ready to be their mother.

I am ready to be a mother. Me. I am ready.

I feel such relief to utter those words I've been longing to speak out as my truth for so long. And finally, it is true. 'I am ready to be a mother.'

Watch out world, for this girl is becoming a woman; this maiden a mother. I am stepping into the boots of motherhood and blazing my own glorious trail!

Right now, I am choosing Love, because I can. I do have the power – to rewrite my story, to author my life, to trust, to face my fears, to dare to love and be loved, to surrender to the graceful flow and abundance of life, to set my heart free!

And the best thing...

It feels so good!

It feels so good to listen to the deep inner knowing... that I am safe, that I am held, that it is okay to Love, that all is well. All is well. All is well in Love.

Now I turn to you, my two precious darlings who came before I was ready. I look at you and I feel such Love for you, the same Love that your newborn brother has set alight in my heart. And I know, just as you know, that my Love for you is enough. I am enough. My Love is enough. Love is always enough.

I look at you, Elijah, my first born – I look at you as you rage, having been exposed to so much of my anger and aggression as I hid my love from you in guard of my heart. I look deep into your eyes and see the fury swelling up amidst the fear (perhaps a reflection of my own journey over the last years). I look at you and I feel such pure, unconditional Love for the boy that you are, just as you are, not needing for you to be anyone else – finally.

And I hold your sister, as she cries, struggling to sleep, weaned from the breast too soon, before she knew how to soothe herself, before she felt safe enough to let go of the day without her mother's milk. I hold her, I hear her pain, and I love her through it all.

All three of you magnificent creatures who I am blessed with the task of mothering – with this newly expanded heart of mine, I promise to love you to the end, so that you may know to your very cores that you are so worthy of being loved. I promise to show up with my Love, day in and day out, through the tears and fears, the fights and sleepless nights, the anger and sorrow, and whatever pain that might come with tomorrow. I will be with you, with Love at our side and all around us, always. That is my promise. I am your mother, now and for always. I am so ready to love you!

DAWN OSABWA

Janet

I wake in the dark and come
to comfort you, the full moon

through the window scuffed
and thin and over-bright,

the nursery as new to me as to you,
our sleepless house a place

where all the women we'll become
gather silently around us,

curious to see what we'll make of this,
our first attempt at love.

SHEILA WILD

'Janet' was first published in the Summer 2016 issue of *JUNO* magazine (issue 44).

Nurturing My Darkness

Take your time and breathe, mama. It's okay. I hear you weeping silently in the dark so as not to wake them. It's been a long day, I know. You've worked hard and they are happy but you're tired. So tired. And the tears come. Don't be scared, I'm here. Just listen.

I know it feels like you're falling apart right now. You are doing this alone with all three. That's tough. You give them your all every moment of every day. Love and safety; warmth and comfort; laughter and joy. You dry every tear. But it's hard. You get to the end of the day and you feel wiped out. The distractions of daytime are gone till the morning and the still of night is setting in. You feel your strength wavering and you're afraid of letting them down. You question your decisions; feel guilty, feel angry, feel sad. Frustrated that you should cope better; you love them so much, they're your world. Your heart sinks and your thoughts become fears. You are alone while they slumber and your night sets in.

You are running on empty my darling. You're struggling but believe me, it's alright. We just need to look after you, and I know you don't feel worthy of that but it's true. I'll tell you why. You are crucially important to this family. The most important in many ways you don't see. You put your children first all the time, in everything you do, because you're their mother and you love them beyond measure. That is a natural perfection right there. But remember that they love you too. Remember that they are here because of you. You grew these beautiful little beings in your body. You nurtured this wondrous vessel of femininity that brought them to life and you have these glorious badges of honour streaked across your belly as an eternal reminder of that. You wear them proudly; be proud of that too.

You cared for your children before they were born by caring for yourself, and it's okay to still do that now. In fact it's essential that you do that now, even though you've lost your way, because they need that too. Honestly, they do. It's not being selfish, you're still putting them first just in a different way. By looking after yourself, doing things you enjoy, giving some love to nourish your own soul, you're refilling your cup to run over once more. And those trickles of your own happiness, that which you've found in yourself, they'll join with the waves of love that radiate from you, relentless and unspoken, and your whole family will drink them in. Think of what a lesson that is, my love. Your little children as adults who know it's good and right to take time for themselves and their spirit. That it benefits everyone. What a loving gift.

Now, I know that it's easy for me to say. I know you feel weak and your confidence is faltering. You keep everything together; everyone where they need to be and doing what they want to do. It's all that you know, but trust me, it's amazing. You give your children a wonderful life and you share their happiness every moment. Let's let them share yours in return. And don't worry, you don't need to know how right now. I'm here, I'll help you. Just start by being kind to yourself. Just try. I know you feel like you're failing but really, you're not. You make mistakes but you're supposed to, you're human, let them go. You want to be the best parent you can be and you strive and strive so very hard for that. But look inside yourself my sweet one, you're already the most perfect parent that your children could ever have because you are you. You're all they want and all they need. Don't underestimate that.

So let's start to dream again, it's been a long time but it'll come. You need to do this for you. You don't have to start big, just a tiny step. Take that bath in the evening when all is quiet, have it as hot as you like. Read. Anything you want. Even a couple of pages while they watch that cartoon you've seen twice already that day. Call your friends. Take up painting. Attempt to teach yourself Mandarin. Alright, back a step. Cook something new. Who knows, after 33 years of avoiding asparagus you might actually love the stuff, and so might the kids. They'll enjoy this too because they'll feel your energy and see that smile. Especially when you put on that song you love and blast it through the kitchen speakers while dancing like a crazy thing. See, there's that smile. So beautiful. Let's start with the little things and we'll go from there. Anything is worth a try.

You are the beating heart of this family, my darling; love emanates from you in every way. You've just got to nurture your reserves somehow, and you deserve to. I know it's tough right now but you're doing so well. Truly you are. Finding love for yourself will only add to the power of the love you give out, so don't despair. You're a wonderful mother, a kind human being, and a perfect you. In time you'll see that again, just like your children see it every day already. It's all they know. They love you so much, just as you are. So keep going. Dry your tears; don't be afraid. Take your time and breathe, mama. You're okay.

DAWN ALLEN

'Nurturing My Darkness' was first published in the Summer 2016 issue of *JUNO* magazine (issue 44).

Water Baby

I saw you first
on the scan
baby swimmer,
echolocation,
two heartbeats,
yours faster than mine.

Mine skipped a beat
at the quickening of you,
when you flipped within me,
whilst singing the songs
of the deep.

You came eagerly,
running the bow wave.
I helped bring you
to the surface,
glistening, warm blooded,
at last, your skin
against mine.

I watched you
take your first breath,
a gasp, no two,
yours and mine,
brought you to my breast,
love at first sight.

Today we run
into the sea together,
dive in and surface laughing.
You, now fully grown,
our two heartbeats,
in time.

KAREN HARVEY

Music

Sometimes in the night,
    I forget you.

Intoxicated on air
perfumed with milk and exhaustion,
we are folded together,
edges filed smooth,
until our boundaries are as blurred
    as yesterday's dreams.

And we flow together like
    music.

JOANNE ADAMS

The Lens of Love

I'm so glad it was me.

I'm glad it wasn't you who slipped on this cold and windswept beach and hit your head on a rock. I'm glad it's not your thoughts that are suddenly thick and fuzzy and it's not your blood that's seeping down your little face or your eye already swelling shut. If it had to be one of us, I'm glad it was me.

When you're hurting, I would take every pinprick and every terrible soreness into my own body if I could save you from the pain.

When you're ill I'd suffer twice the sickness and twice the unpleasantness, just to give you back your energy and your spark.

When you're sad I would hold you in my arms and lock your tears away in my own aching heart if it would help you smile again.

But then how would you learn, and grow, and find your own inner strength and resilience?

Watching you grow up so very, very fast, I long to wrap you in the warm, soft blanket of my love, to protect you and keep you safe forever. Loving you as I do, instead I teach myself to step aside as you venture forwards, testing, trying, discovering – strong and sure of yourself. I hold the blanket ready to warm you when you ask – but I will not smother your vitality with it.

Looking at your face through the lens of love, I see every layer of you: the tiny baby with needs so ferocious and all-consuming; the toddler growing more sure-footed and talkative by the hour; the young child full of questions and giggles and endless fascination with the world. But I remind myself time and again that you see only now. For you, who you are and what you feel at this second is all there has ever been. For me, who you are, what you express and what you need changes moment by moment – and so I step back and listen carefully, careful not to respond to the you of yesterday, instead of the you standing in front of me today.

Learning with you, I see that even as an infant, only you could live your life. I could play, feed, warm, and soothe, but the feelings and experiences – joy, hunger, cold, overwhelming emotion – could only ever be yours.

How can I protect you from harm without shielding you from life itself?

When you're hurting, I will listen and tend your wounds, and let you heal yourself.

When you're ill I will give you the best of care, and help you to nurture yourself.

When you're sad I will offer all the comfort I can, and hold my own tears deep inside so you never feel you need to comfort me or hide your feelings.

When you're grown and flown, I will celebrate your independence – and looking back through the lens of love, I will remember this rocky beach and still be glad that today, the pain was mine.

I'm so glad you're safe.

LIZ PROCTOR

Belly

I never liked it.

Since giving birth
there is no chance of fixing it.

No amount of exercise
will remove the pannus,
the wrinkly sac that
hangs and sways and folds.

It swings free of me,

has taken on a life of its own.

My one year old son just found it,
slapped it joyously with both hands and
plunged his face into it with gay abandon.

He blows and laughs as the raspberries resound.

I am slick with spit,
babyslimed
from ribcage to pant line.

He pulls himself up me,
slips and dives,
wriggles and writhes,
enjoying himself so much
I needn't continue to laugh.

I just watch,
amazed and delighted.

When he finally rests,
drifts off to sleep smiling,
I tuck my tummy away
with a friendly pat.

CLAIRE STEPHENSON

Love Is...

Love is when he...

...mispronounces the word 'complluter'. And a sadness in you when he starts saying it properly.

...says 'I'm going to make you breakfast, Mummy,' when you're ill in bed. And then says, crestfallen, 'I can't reach the bowls, Mummy.'

...holds up Little Ted to the bus window so teddy can see out and also enjoy the ride

...reprimands the bus driver for going so slowly. 'Hurry up, bus driver! My Mummy's going to be late for EastEnders.' You tell him it's not on today so he snaps louder. 'Hurry up, bus driver! I'm going to be late for... for... for my toys!' You see the lady's shoulders in the seat in front shaking up and down.

...belly laughs when watching *Mr Bean*; dimples in his cheeks, pinpointing his joy. No sense of having to hold it in. You can't either.

...shouts, 'There are two Aidens, Mummy,' when he meets someone with his name.

...says sadly, 'Will I go to prison, Mummy?' when he shared his cheese and ham sandwich with his Muslim friend.

Love is when you...

...hold his warm, little hand in yours as you walk to the bus stop.

...hug him tight, reassuring him that Nicole Kidman in the film *Paddington* doesn't live in your London.

...feel his hot, light breath against your skin when you cuddle up in bed.

...push him on the swing for the hundredth time, watching him smile.

...run up and down a muddy, grass bank in the freezing cold, trying to get his kite to fly.

...queue up in McDonalds for his Happy Meal, your nerves jangling from the noise.

...have his friends over, leaving a trail of chaos over your living room floor.

...keep all his 'art' work since nursery days in your overfilled storage cupboard.

...play I Spy for hours on end and the objects are not even in sight.

...walk up and down the swimming bath, holding him afloat.

...read him a bedtime story; he falls asleep curled up against your middle-aged spread.

NICKY TORODE

Forever Love

Love is nice,
Love is calm.
Love is trustworthy,
Love goes far.

Love is trust,
Love carries on.
Love is wonderful,
Love is great.

Love is help,
Love is beyond words.
Love is clever,
Love shows emotion,
It helps bonds form forever.

I. RAWLINSON (9 years old)

An Austin Morning

On a morning in Austin
I feel warm and cozy in my bed. I can hear the wind howling.
Downstairs my grandmother and grandfather greet me
With a bowl of cereal for breakfast.
I walk outside, leaves crunching under my feet
While a cat named Feathers
Darts inside the house
As fast as a cougar
And up the stairs, under the couch with Bazar, the other cat.
I follow Feathers back in
To ring the morning bell.
My brother zips out of the room
Like a shotgun bullet.
Running downstairs three at a time.
We all meet in the kitchen where my grandfather
Is making eggs.
I look around the room at all my family members
Surrounding me in a blanket of love.
I feel safe and calm.
Brown is the color of coziness and safeness.
It is the color of an Austin morning.

ALEX HABEEB (9 years old)

Sisters

The laughter escapes from her lips,
Vibrant and enticing,
As her childish feet,
Caress along the sofa.
She lays not a care in the world.
Nothing may penetrate her bubble,
Our bubble,
Of exhilaration.

We are one,
Her fingers slip into mine,
And we radiate the same elation.
As we prance in our euphoria
And reign in the kingdom of happiness
That thrives beneath our hands,
And our hearts.
It is enchanting.

We unite,
Under the stars,
Under the magic,
And under the felicity,
Of our love.

CHARVI JAIN (13 years old)

Get Along

Time ticks by
And my anger swells,
Then I go tell.
My brother says, 'Tattletale!'
He cries, 'Boohoo!'
My mom says, 'That's not
The right thing to do.'
So I say sorry, and
We all say, 'Woohoo!'

And after that
I stop being a brat,
And think about
What family is.
Family is a big keepsake.
Family is a wonderful thing.
Family takes care of you,
So you take care of it, too.

TIFFANY 'TJ' MCREYNOLDS (9 years old)

Lanora's Love Poem

Granddad makes me nice chocolate milkshakes
And I like the taste of them
I love eating chocolate cake
I love my mummy
Love is a kind thing
What's your favourite thing?

LANORA CLARKE (5 years old)

Why I write poetry (To Dad)

I love you and you love me,
You fill my life with joy and glee.
You are the sun that lights my day,
You're always there when I want to play.
I love you and you love me —
YOU are why I write poetry.

RUBY LAMEY SARKAR (9 years old)

Love Ain't Enough

I kind of hate the word love. When I hear it it sounds trite, vague and overloaded with sentiment. For me, love is out of fashion. If you can use it as an adjective for anything from a prawn ring to a pair of shoes then it's definitely not got the heavy-weight clout I'm looking for. I need something to describe the earth-shifting, nausea-inducing, simply unfathomable feeling that forced me to redefine myself, my life and my vocabulary when our two became three.

It wasn't enough to describe what happened when I relented to falling for my best friend two years ago either. When Jamie and I decided to stop holding hands in the playground and put an official *and* between our names I had to confront something entirely unexpected, which was that (and forgive me for sounding so unwantingly "profound") he was my *soul mate...* wait, my soul mate? Hang on whilst I cringe at myself. Reader, stay with me here.

What I'm looking for is a love PR guru. A family portrait that isn't contrived smiles in matching denim against a white background. A way to avoid the inevitable matching anorak situation that seems to blight every once trendy couple who now seem to believe that dressing the five-year-old in the same Peter Storm as Mummy and Daddy is akin to hoisting the family crest over the threshold.

What I need is a new vocabulary. 'Love' and 'Soul Mate' have been diluted, whitewashed. They're pre-watershed descriptions. My love for my pseudo-husband (more than a boyfriend but without the ring to prove it) is explicit; it should have parental advisory plastered all over it, I shouldn't even be allowed to mention it in front of my Grandmother else she wash my mouth out with soap. At the same time though it's delicate, wistful, ridiculous, childlike, innocent... it feels like no one has ever been in love like this before and no one can possibly be in love like this after. All this, but at the same time spectacularly lacking in its uniqueness. And this is just a human to human connection. How can I even quantify the love for my baby?

Let's just park 'love' for a minute and allow me to describe what happened when that double blue line appeared in front of my eyes. First, you need to know something about me. I don't take exaggeration lightly. In fact I baulk so highly at someone's suggestion that 'you've got to try this coffee shop, they do the *best* coffee cake ever!' that I will, out of spite, not just **not** try the cake, I also will not try the "amazing" flat white, the 'awesome' ham and emmenthal toasty, heck I won't even go to the shop itself, all due to your completely unquantifiable over-exaggeration. To be honest, my opinion would be so catastrophically and irreparably diminished I will be forced to not take you seriously again. *Ever.*

With that in mind, when I found out my belly was now home to a five-week-old example of cell division, I am fairly certain that the world stopped, reset its rotation sequence and began spinning in the opposite direction. From there my baby began its lifetime of teaching me how to be a better human. Before she was born, Indigo forced me to confront every fear that had before now kept me shy of confrontation, unsure of my decisions and unable to trust my intuition. She showed me I was capable of unimaginable strength of mind. I have dug my heels in every step of the way when it has come to making decisions that affect her wellbeing, from birthing at home to the odd sensation of being in such emotional and physical pain in the early stages of breastfeeding that I could do nothing but cry my exhausted tears to release the frustration, only to watch them land on her contented, suckling, strange little face and see in their sparkling reflection a face that was never going to be any good to helping her feel secure. I couldn't let that despair be part of her happy meal. So I curled my toes instead and sent the pain out through my feet. Eventually I stopped having to curl my toes and it started to look like the scenes in the breastfeeding pamphlets, all soft glow and gentle contentment. But it was only love that made me do it.

It's this kind of love that makes me jump out of bed at 3:30 a.m. when her feverish cries pierce that all too unfamiliar and undisturbed sleep. It makes me come close to wetting myself when she falls asleep in my arms but I can't bring myself to put her down and disturb her rest. It makes her milky sick breath smell like you could bottle it and flog it as Beyoncé's new fragrance (to me, anyway). But most of all, it makes every difficult task devoid of resentment towards that helpless little genius. It keeps me calm... okay, mostly keeps me calm. I'm no martyr here.

So you see, this is why I'm quite unsatisfied with this singularly ordinary word that gets bandied around day to day, espoused in fake American accents by homogenised pop starlets in every other chart hit. It isn't the same feeling I know, you couldn't cover it in diamanté and plaster it on a t-shirt. It's so much more than that. When people ask me how it has been since we had a baby, I say it's like being in the eye of a storm. Chaos could be raging but with that kid in your arms you suddenly just... are. You exist. And you just quite don't know how but you *love* every second.

SARAH WILLIS

Love and Home Education

Me

Standing on High Tor, tall and alone, tears well at the corners of my eyes. The earth shifts beneath my feet as I make a momentous decision; *I am going to home educate my son.* I quietly offer my pledge to the heavens, repeating the words like a mantra, the houses and fields blurring below me as tears begin to fall. I feel like a traitor, swimming against the tide of my own kin and society, yet I must walk this new path on the extraordinary journey of motherhood. I exhale deeply, relief washing over me. It – is – done. I turn away, walking down the hill breathing in, 'I am more than ready and qualified to do this,' breathing out: 'I know this to be right.'

I am on another exhilarating walk in the Dark Peak, my baby daughter strapped firmly to my back. Vast open spaces offer me time to reflect. My heart pulses to the fluctuating rhythms of the seasons; the wind, rain and sun bright, harsh and refreshing on my face, whipping, bleaching and wetting my hair, feeding my soul. I thank Mother Earth for the gift of time in this wild landscape. Here I can really think. I march, stroll and run as I seek answers to the question, *How should my son be educated?*

My Grandfather

I feel your absence weighing me down as your great grandchild grows within me. I snatch at half-remembered stories of your life gathered from childhood. If only I had discovered more. As I plant roots in our new home, I mourn your death; the loss of a grandfather never known. My family paint you as a deeply religious man with strong convictions and a creative spirit, a conscientious objector, peacemaker and vegetarian. I sense a note of disapproval as my mother, your daughter, describes you, yet I feel a deep connection with your unorthodoxy. You are my kindred spirit from beyond the grave, where I seek communion with you.

Would you have supported our parenting decisions more than my own parents have? Have character traits bypassed a generation? Am I more like you than I am my own parents?

I know you would have embraced our unconventional parenting choices, which comforts me. Granddad, I wish I could have met you.

My Grandmother

Standing in the nursing home, you hold my hands tightly, look me straight in the eye and say, 'Look after him, Caroline.' Nodding, I fight back tears, before losing you again to dementia. I hold onto these lucid moments as precious offerings, blessed you knew I was pregnant. Two months later you are gone. Your ninth great-grandchild is newly born, life and death met from both sides. I hope I am living out your request as best I can, my dear Nanna. I feel your presence in the clouds, the hills, the stars, as a whisper on the wind as I walk with my son. Your love and approval are constant.

My Father

We converse late into the night, you and Mum trying to convince me not to home educate. When I eventually go to bed I toss and turn, words swimming round my head as an abyss opens inside me. Four years later, the pit is hollow and cold, your disapproval solid and unwavering. My desperation for approval from you is a tiny burning flame of hope that perhaps one day you will support our decision. Set me free, allow me to truly find my own path in life. To love someone is to truly let them go. I know this is so hard to do. I ache for your blessing in my choices, I long to share with you our exploits, our learning, for you to join in. Instead there is silence or sudden outbursts.

Your concern springs purely out of unconditional love for your first-born grandchild; you wish for him to have as "normal" a childhood as possible, protecting him from the alienating feelings of difference which plagued you as a child. I must learn to accept your disapproval instead of wasting energy fighting against it.

My family

I announce our decision to home educate at a family meal. A sudden barrage of negatives pierce the air like arrows fired directly at me:

It is child abuse. I hope you don't have another child. Don't experiment with your son's education. You are setting him up for failure. He will always feel different. What makes you think you are better than other people?

Stinging and broken I retreat confused, wondering if I can face the uphill struggle to come. Silence and denial follow. Doubts lingering, we enrol our son in school. We eat and sleep a nightmare as our request for him to attend part time is refused. Sitting in the Head's office, I am a child again, dis-empowered, cowering to The System. The Head holds up her hands, shakes her head and admits her school is more important than our son. The next day we withdraw our son from school before he even started. We return to the path we almost took...

Society

Finding our feet in this new world I hold my head high, replying to queries about my son with conviction, looking people in the eye. *My son is home educated.* My son is blossoming, happy, his life full, varied and rich. I seek out families who share our ethos; parents who wish to be with their children, allowing them time to play, explore and learn in nature, to simply be children without the dominance of electronic gadgetry. For our children's creativity to emerge and their souls to shine, we feel we must take this drastic step. We are worried about the direction our state education system is heading and are frustrated by a lack of alternative provision. We have voted with our feet by educating our children "otherwise". Our decision is not taken lightly.

My son

On one of our many walks you hunt for boggart homes in the boughs of trees, offer your sister fairy cups from the forest floor, ponder why the leaves have fallen from the trees and whether there is gravity in space. I treasure this time with you, these moments of togetherness when I see you learning. It is a true privilege to be present as you make new discoveries. Your curiosity is infectious, your unquenchable desire to learn astounding. Home education can be challenging, but it is never boring. In our countless adventures you are as much my teacher as I am yours. I am young again, I see life through a new lens, I pause to really look.

In the rhythm of our days you spend little time formally learning, spending time in nature, in groups and in the community. Home education has given us six weeks trekking in Nepal, with another big trip planned in the autumn, as well as countless smaller adventures in the foreground. We embrace the challenge home education brings as you enter your seventh year. I thank you for allowing me to share the first years of your life beside you. Here's to the next seven...

Ewan, know I home educate you because I love you deeply, my child, no matter what.

CAROLINE COLE

Anything Could Happen

After 'Anything Can Happen in this Poem'
by Heather Summerhayes Cariou.

Sophie has an incredible vocabulary... and a condition called Selective Mutism. She can draw beautiful pictures and sing with the voice of an angel... and in an instant she is screaming obscenities and threats and pain and fear.

Her imagination soars, her eyes shine, her laughter delights... and then a simple request and that thing they call Obsessive Compulsive Disorder rears its ugly head and the air is filled with her rigid and unyielding tenacity. The struggle ensues, the fight for control.

I might stay calm this time, grasping for the tools I've been taught to use. I might divert the storm. I might not.

Magic could happen. Sophie could wake one morning and suddenly be "typical", moving through her day with the carefree ease of any other first grader. Magic could happen. Please God.

My daughter is highly intelligent, beautiful, talented and struggling. And in my frustration and despair, I desperately want to like her more.

We could try another medication, another therapy, another approach. She's nearly seven and I cringe at the thought of her at sixteen. We move through the days, months, years with the unpredictability of the ocean. Some days we float on calm waters. Most days we fight the rough seas.

We forge on, we do it fiercely and we do it together.

DEBORAH L. STAUNTON

Josef

– the foot that stirred under my heart
rests now, a fingertip length, on its
white shroud. My nestling,
your neck is a daisy stem
your uncurled hand a starfish
beached. Eyes sealed now
against discovery

of ribbed wet sand
the suck and pull of waves
the beat of rain
and sweet milk mouthful.

We will make
a wonky cross of bluebells
for your sister to carry.
Your brother will hold
the small white box
close to his chest
behind your dad
along the woodland path
where kind trees will
shelter you

and us as the rain falls
and the waves try to pull us under.

MAEVE HENRY

Poem for Imogen

The beat that came too late for life
A missed pulse
A stilled heart
A silent pause in the delivery room's bustle.

A mother
With empty arms
And aching breasts
Whose heart will always beat with love for this baby.

A grandmother and great-grandmother who wait
With aching arms
And pricked fingers that have pieced and pierced
Quilted and stitched
Knitted and sewed
In preparation for this baby
Who skipped a vital beat and slipped away
A dropped stitch in time.

ANN ABINERI

Ashes

On All Hallows' Day, we finally scattered the ashes of my paternal grandmother who had passed away the previous October. For a year her ashes (well, actually half of them – not relevant here) had sat on my parent's mantelpiece becoming a kind of comforting ancestral presence in the house where both my parents would speak to her. The reason for the long wait was that my sister lives in America and this was the first time since the funeral that she had been home.

I was six months pregnant when my grandmother died. I was sad that she did not get to meet Baby E but was grateful that perhaps Baby E had heard her voice or in some way had been around her. My grandmother had had Alzheimer's, which developed quickly after my grandfather had died, so in her final years she lived in a wonderful care home not far from where she grew up and had lived all of her life. It was here that we told her over several visits about me being pregnant, it was here that she asked me, 'What you going to call her?' which convinced me that my little boy was going to be a little girl, and it was here that she died, surrounded by people who loved her.

I was there the night she died, though the whole process unfolded over a few days. It was a sad but remarkable experience, and I felt privileged to be able to help hold a safe space in which she could leave. During the final visits before the Friday that she died my father, my mother and I would sit with my grandmother as she lay in her bed. She was no longer in a place of talking but would intermittently squeeze our hands. We knew that she was leaving. We would talk to her and also talk about her life and memories that we had. We imagined her as a girl, a young woman and wondered about the things about her life that we would never know. A few times we sang some of her favourite songs including *Goodnight My Love* by Ella Fitzgerald, a hugely appropriate song for parting, and which she had also sung to my grandfather as he lay dying ten years earlier.

When we had exhausted our (shaky) repertoire I played a song from my phone. It was a piece that I had happened to come across around that time and had been playing to Baby E by placing headphones on my tummy, and thought that it would have been something that my grandmother would have liked. The piece was *Spiegel im Spiegel* by Estonian composer Arvo Part. I have since learned that this is a popular choice at funerals and it is easy to understand why. Translated as *Mirror in Mirror* the piano and cello piece opens up a vast imaginative space for conjuring images. For me it created a space to think about my relationship with my grandmother and helped me say goodbye – though as she suffered from Alzheimer's we had in many ways been losing her for the past few years. Since then I have tried to play the piece as a way of re-entering that time and to think about my grandmother, but each time I have had to switch it off, it being so powerful in its evocation. Even recently when I walked into our living room and it happened to be playing on the radio I caught my breath as I was instantly transported again to my grandmother's bedside during those final days. What I noticed when we played this music to my grandmother was that she appeared to become more restful. Before that she had been moving her arms a lot, touching her head and face, but with the piano music playing she became less fidgety, more still. I like to think that she felt comforted, though of course I cannot truly know.

So during those last visits my parents and I would sing and talk to each other. Sometimes Baby E would kick, reminding me that I was witness to the threshold between life and death, and remembering the phrase 'one in one out' (or in our case one in, two out as my maternal grandmother also died days before Baby E was born) as one generation was leaving and one was getting ready to arrive. But mostly, and what I will always remember about this time, we sat in silence, holding vigil, listening to this piece of music on repeat and allowing it to weave us together in order to say goodbye.

Many months and one baby later my father, my mother, my sister, my partner and my eight-month-old son climb the side of a waterfall. We carry my grandmother's ashes and a bunch of flowers picked from our garden. My partner carries Baby E on his back in the baby carrier. We were returning to the site where we had scattered my grandfather's ashes ten years before. Like our own worlds the landscape of this place, which had been significant to my grandfather, had changed. The stone where my sister had planted a flower was now overgrown. For some of us, well maybe all of us, the climb was much steeper – except for Baby E who was experiencing it for the first time.

It was a beautiful bright autumnal day and though by chance the timing of our family ritual on All Hallows Day seemed hugely fitting. Especially pertinent was the pagan tradition of celebrating the dead, commemorating the beginning of a new year and also welcoming into the community children who had been born during the past few months. Although Baby E was of course too young to understand why we were there, he offered comfort and lightness in his babblings and in his embodiment of the future.

We decorated the stone with the flowers, imbued now with family significance, and each took it in turn to scatter the ashes. My sister and I started to gently sing *Goodnight My Love* (my sister leading, as she is the better singer) and we shared some memories of my grandmother. It was not sombre. There was laughter but also quiet moments. At some points during the silence we could hear the crisp leaves from a nearby tree falling. I sat on a soft, slightly damp, mound of grass to breastfeed Baby E. When all of my grandmother's ashes had been released out into the whirling autumnal air to join the river, the soil, the trees and plants we descended the steep climb and returned back home.

FERN THOMAS

My Turn

Deep night shifts shudders.
Dad's defiant lungs creak, cracking
silence. A sentinel night-light keeps
scattered focus sharp.

Rafters sigh with burdens. Foxed
memories lie folded in tissue. The room
waits for a steady rhythm, holds stale breath.
Outside neon streetlights flicker.

His bedroom's now a Cabinet of Curiosities,
bedside table a pharmaceutical clutter,
hunched in the corner, the arachnid zimmer.
Unworn orthopedic shoes lie redundant.

Soft white cotton slides on mottled skin.
Bed rails jangle as chicken-bone knuckles
grasp in the dark. Dad's skeletal head swivels
seeking the amethyst gift-wrapped hyacinths.

I hold his hand, begin to sing.

FINOLA SCOTT

The Laughing Day, the Hours of Breathing

From the hospital I could just hear
children laughing at play – the only time
of life when screams signify fun.

My focus, though, was the mouth
of my father in the spotless bed.
His lungs were an orchestra tuning up,
his flickering tongue conducting
the bass rasps and grunts of effort.
It went on forever, though I knew
that it would stop today.

Today, this day, this bright midsummer morning,
the flowers have been dancing in their best clothes.
Even the trees have on full shimmering coats,
squirrels rummaging in the pockets.
The birdsong is surely all laughter,
any fighting an am-dram re-enactment
for the pleasures of costume and action.

My father's beard should be blossoms
or feathers, not snow. It moves to the clumsy,
clunky clockwork of lung-time.
The longest day. A day not to forget.
A beautiful time to die.
The day that stays with me, summer rivers
running softly with my tears.

CATHY BRYANT

The Miracle of Love

The happiest day of my life was when my father died.

Strange really when I had always been afraid of death. Yet with my father, death was a constant companion, standing just in the background, waiting patiently for him.

It was hard, because Dad refused to play nicely. He was cheating death. Still death remained, part of our family, travelling with us on holiday, to weddings and even other people's funerals.

Dad hung on, stuck in a fragile body held together by sheer will.

'You're only twenty Tracey, it's my duty to take care of you till you are old enough to fend for yourself.'

Dad had come out of hospital. Death felt closer, we could not push him away.

I had arrived home from college late. As I entered Dad's cough broke the silence, dry, and rasping from his gut. I turned on my record player, to drown out the noise; I could not bear to hear him in so much pain.

I slowly changed my clothes, and slumped across the bed, running my fingers across a record sleeve. I found a Eurhythmics' song; its lyrics complemented my mood. I lay back and stared up at the ceiling, watching the lights from my wind chimes dance on the white walls.

Living in a flat meant that you are never far away from noises, Dad coughed again as he rose, the shuffle of his feet echoed as he crossed the room. I turned the music up and began to sing.

The miracle of love. Will take away your pain.

I lifted myself off the bed and walked into the kitchen.

Mum was cooking tea, a frown on her face. We all shared

that look lately; it was as if a veil of unhappiness had settled over our family.

'Are you hungry?'

I shrugged.

Mum frowned again, the lines on her face made more visible. I could see new ones had appeared, more pronounced.

I sat in the seat across from Dad. He was staring out of the window, not at anything in particular, just out across the field and beyond.

'Tracey, good day?'

I nodded. He sighed then turned back to the window and his thoughts. I sat curled up in the chair, staring at my hands, tracing the deep lines. My lifeline was long; my Dad's was long too. Definitely someone's idea of a cosmic joke.

Grabbing the newspaper, I began flipping through the pages. Dad stood up and began to walk towards the settee. Both Mum and I ran over to help him. We settled him as comfortable as possible, still he seemed so small, shrivelled up. He slumped onto the cushion and took a deep breath, still it did not seem enough, he gasped again drawing air deeply into his worn lungs, and his eyes closed.

Mum phoned the doctor. The Doctor was busy saying she would get here when she had the time. So we waited.

Mum went into the kitchen, to escape the coarse rattle coming from Dad, and I sat across from him and tried to breathe for him.

Dad's breathing slowed, became shallow, less strained. I sat in silence, watching the rhythm alter, then slowly cease. I was glad. I stood up and walked over to where Dad lay, a smile on his face, the pain gone, leaving him relaxed, free.

'Rest now Dad, I will be fine.'

I felt myself smile, as I reached to touch his face.

We all mourned, not only for Dad but for death too. He

had become a part of our life. I wish I could have thanked him, because this time he had shown both of us mercy.

TRACEY HOLLAND

Valentine's Day

Valentine's Day was liver coloured
a semi-transparent parcel
that slid onto the palm
wet with deceit and drama.

Valentine's Day was a Triumph Herald engine
turning over and puttering away.
A propelling-pencil gift
that couldn't compensate for losing a father.

Age 11 didn't feel the attraction
of the deep well.
Didn't want to touch the cold sides
on the way to the bottom.

Age 11 poured glue in the kiln and blew up the pots
stole trainer bras from Lewis's
fake jewelry and gonks
tipped over school desks and dropped tampons
from trees
bullied classmates for money
talked cider and sex
loved art and Mr Grundy
football and fires
craved pot noodles and Pernod
and Marlboro lights.

Age 11 wanted to make complicated sweet jar mazes
to house locusts and stick insects
with Dad
forever.

KAREN LITTLE

Mother's Day

'Your ears should be burning,' I say, staring at her photo. 'We did nothing but talk about you all day. Nice stuff of course, and we had such a laugh. Funny that, because to be honest Mum, I didn't think I would laugh ever again, especially today of all days. Believe me I was all set to cancel and yes I do know it's not THE day, but the girls insisted. Mother's Day was always special. I'd take you for lunch and then we'd come back here and have tea with the girls, but then you spoilt all that last year, didn't you?

'I was so angry with you. I never said. But you knew, I could tell. It was like when I was little. Do you remember when I'd have a strop over something stupid? You'd be there waiting for me to calm down and then you'd hug me. Even years later when HE had one too many dalliances, as you used to call them, and I kicked him out for good you never once said "I told you so". I'm rambling but I have to get this off my chest. You see I'm sorry. Sorry all I could think about last year was how I'd feel every Mother's Day without you, and sorry it's taken me the year to appreciate how, as you lost your fight to beat that evil disease, you rose to the ultimate challenge and make everything all right for me.

'Today with my girls and our memories I understood your final act of love. I miss you terribly Mum, and wish with all my heart you were here with me, but I am ready to face the future.

'Let me explain.

'You always said the girls would look after me. Well, they took me out for lunch today. It's what Grandma would have wanted, they told me. They left an hour ago and once I'd arranged their flowers I poured a glass of wine and got out this photo of you. Not the best, I know and I'm sorry about that but the cancer had already got a grip. Anyway, you never liked having your picture taken, did you? Still, you are smiling so I used it for the order of service, hope you don't mind.

'Oh and since it is Mother's Day I'm drinking Chablis. I thought you'd approve. We always treated ourselves on special days, didn't we? And today is extra special. I can now make sense of your final weeks and know you were truly at peace in the end. I see you smile knowingly, ready to nod in agreement, but I want to tell you anyway.

'Today we relived your final day, and oh, how privileged I feel to have shared every moment. But one thing still bugs me. How did you know you were going to die that day?

'The nurse phoned after seven in the morning. She said you were asking for me.

'"Don't be sad, Laura," you told me before the morphine kicked in.

'"What's the date?" you asked, and I answered, telling you it was Mother's Day too. I could see in your eyes you understood that bit. No, it was the date you'd forgotten and that was important. You always were a stickler for dates. Birthdays, anniversaries, you name it you'd remember and on this day you had to know for completeness, the date of your death. I understood. I also recalled our conversation the day before.

'You told me the dream you'd had about your funeral and who was there and what the weather was like. There was a good turnout you said, everyone did you proud. Not sure about what I was wearing, you said. I should think again. I tried not to cry, but you were so matter-of-fact. Were we going to have sherry and wine at the "do" afterwards, you were eager to know, fretting we might suggest a teetotal affair. You wanted it to be a party like those we had to celebrate your special birthdays, you said, even if you had to give this one a miss. You hadn't lost your wicked sense of humour either, had you? So for the record I'll tell you now, we didn't allow Uncle Sam to play the organ. You were adamant about that, weren't you? You said he'd messed up at my wedding.'

'But let me get back to your final day.

'I remember studying your gaunt face and scrutinising your features for a hint of what was going through your mind. You squeezed my hand and reluctantly I shared your calm acceptance of the inevitable. The moment passed. I got up and busied myself arranging the daffodils I'd brought for you for Mother's Day, as always. Each year we'd marvel at how long they lasted, each new bud opening to reveal the magnificent trumpet. The first sign of spring, we'd agree, and the promise of warmer days ahead. But that final display of golden glory would pass you by.

'Again I turned to look at you. Anger no longer howled at me from your tired blue eyes. In its place I recognised the warmth I'd always known, and that mischievous twinkle which was undeniably you, Mum, before you got ill.

'And then the girls arrived. We stood round you like characters in some bizarre farce, making polite conversation as we watched and waited, and you, with your understated sense of humour sharpened in spite of the morphine, or perhaps because of it, took centre stage.

'"I'll probably keep you waiting," you announced, your voice strong, unfaltering. And we laughed nervously as you began to recount stories of your past; reminding us of your impending end. Time passed. You tired, drifting in and out of consciousness and we watched, expectantly, but your heart was strong.

'"I'm dead!" you shouted, sitting bolt upright. Surveying the sea of faces, recognition dawned and you fell against the pillows with a wry smile on your face, "Not yet," you whispered. You were in a world of your own, going back over your life. We remained at your bedside. You shared our laughter and our tears, but then as morning became afternoon and the watery March sunshine began to fade, your mind became muddled.'

'I blamed the drugs. It was kinder than facing up to the truth. We lost you soon afterwards. I knew you'd gone when your eyes flickered and closed, even though your beating heart and laboured breathing remained for some time before your body finally succumbed, and the eerie silence of death stole the moment.

'I cried. You'd left me, and on Mother's Day. How could you? But now, one year on, I treasure your last day.

'"Don't be sad, Laura," you told me in that lucid moment at the beginning of the day. And now I understand. You were selflessly preparing me for tomorrow and the next day, and the day after that. Thank you, Mum. You have made everything all right once again, and with my girls I'll preserve our tradition and celebrate Mother's Day in the usual way every year.'

RACHEL NEWMAN

I Measure My Mother's Love

In spools of thread:
royal blue Sylko and scarlet Gütermann.
In sixpenny cards of buttons:
pink and blue for handknit cardis,
plain white for cuffed school shirts,
turquoise florins for my sister's coat.
In bolts of cloth tied with string:
polished cotton for summer frocks,
brushed Viyella for winter nightgowns,
grey twill for press-pleated skirts.

In rustless needles and blood-sharp pins,
in running stitches tacking shapeless fabric
to lithesome bodies and coltish limbs,
in smocking and twice-sewn French seams,
in the electric hum of the black and gold Singer,
in turned hems, let down as we grew.

ANGI HOLDEN

Their House is a Slipper

Their house is a slipper, I step inside
and it brings the comfort of a cup of tea.
Burgundy warms me and I squeeze
onto the slightly-too-small sofa
as my Nan animates like a TV presenter
telling us stories with a smile, laughter contagious,
punctuating her sentences with our names.

Would you believe it Mark?
Andrea, do you ever find that...?
It's got to be a genuine reduction Carmina.

My Grandad raises up on his toes
to kiss me on the forehead,
then takes position in his armchair,
reeling off the odd joke or two.
Did I ever tell you the one
about the woman who wore a cat on her head?

My Nan potters about in the kitchen taking drink orders,
the wooden rumble of the pantry door slides open
for Hob-Nobs and Digestives. She dishes them out,
telling us to remember everything in moderation,
despite her not ever being able to make a box of chocolates
last more than one day.

CARMINA MASOLIVER

My Gadabout Gran

My Gran was a Gadabout. At least that's what Mum and Dad said. The first time I heard one of them say it I looked it up in the dictionary we keep on the kitchen dresser. It said 'Someone who travels about seeking pleasure; a social butterfly.' I didn't really understand how Gran could be a butterfly but I thought it might be because she fluttered into our house wearing beautiful scarves.

Grandad died a long time ago, before I can remember, and Gran lived on her own. She had lots of friends who she met for lunch or for the theatre. Every summer she would Gadabout with her friends. I heard Dad say to Mum 'She's got a new lease of life' and that sounded a happy thing. I thought it might be to do with her being a butterfly.

Gran would bring back things from her Gadding trips. Sometimes they were presents, like rainbow juggling balls from Notting Hill Carnival for Dad or fairy wings from Glastonbury for my Mum. She brought me amazing things, like a rain stick that was made from cactus and had rattling beans inside and a Russian doll where each doll had a president's face. Sometimes the things she brought back were for her house, like the scary wooden mask she put on her downstairs loo wall. I always went upstairs to the bathroom after that. On another trip Gran bought herself a scarf with rows of shiny metal discs to wear for her belly dancing classes at the Community Centre.

One spring Gran went away for a long trip. Mum and Dad called it a Road Trip, which I thought was a bit funny because all trips involve roads. Even when you fly in a plane to a holiday place, there's always a road when you get there. Well perhaps not in the jungle but I didn't think Gran and her friends were going to a jungle. They were going to drive around Eastern Europe looking for Flea Markets.

'I hope we find some real markets,' said Gran. 'Like they used to have in Paris and Amsterdam. Full of treasures looking for a new home, no mass produced tat.'

'Heaven forbid you should buy any tat,' said my Dad and winked at me. Mum gave him one of her looks.

Gran did come back with treasure that summer: old books written in alphabets that I couldn't read, an armadillo shell that didn't have an armadillo inside it anymore and a glass paperweight shaped like a real skull. I was a bit disappointed that Gran didn't bring back any fleas but she did bring butterflies.

The butterflies were inside a framed box. After I had been watching them for a while, Gran explained that they had died before they were put in there. I looked again and could see that they were pinned neatly to the back of the box. Each one had a name written alongside it although the ink had almost faded away. Orange Albatross. Magpie Crow. Autumn Leaf. I was fascinated by these names and I loved the butterflies' coloured wings. Gran put them on the wall next to her favourite chair. 'They lived in India before they ended up in a glass case in a market in Budapest,' she explained. 'I love to picture them fluttering around in the sunshine.'

That summer I noticed that Gran was spending more time sitting in her favourite chair and less time Gadding About. I think Mum and Dad were worried too. Sometimes when we went round she was dozing in her chair, her glasses resting on the latest travel agency brochure. One day it was a brochure for India. 'Not sure if I'll get there now,' said Gran.

One Monday morning, when the weather was getting cooler, Gran had a Fall. Dad said that when the ambulance came to take her to hospital, the paramedic phoned ahead and said Gran was Off Her Legs.

We went to visit Gran once they'd got her Settled. To visit

her you had to go past lots of rooms, each one with an ill person in it. We took her travel books to read when she felt a bit better. Books about Assam, Uttar Pradesh and Kerala. She thanked us but seemed very tired.

On Friday Dad and Mum picked me up from school together and, as I crunched slowly towards them through the leaves that had blown across the playground, I knew from their faces that they had something sad to say. Mum crouched down and took my hands in hers then said quietly that Gran had died. We went home and Dad made us cheese on toast, which he said was Comfort Food, and we played quiet card games all evening.

The next morning when I woke up I found it hard to believe it was true. I asked Mum if we could visit Gran's house to see if she was there. Mum explained that Gran wouldn't be there, as she was at the hospital waiting for a Funeral, but we could go to the house if I wished as there were Things To Do. She said it might be nice if I chose something of Gran's to keep.

When we got there I went straight over to Gran's favourite chair. The small table had been tipped over and some of Gran's belongings were on the floor. The butterfly case was face down amongst them.

I picked it up carefully. The glass was still intact but the case was a bit damaged at the back. Two butterflies remained in their places but one neatly written label only had a pin hole next to it.

Mum and I searched for the third butterfly but it wasn't there. Mum seemed surprised that I still wanted to take the butterflies home. I held the damaged case carefully on my lap in the car and when we got home dad mended the back with tape and put it up in the spot I had chosen.

My bedroom has been decorated twice since then but I always ask Dad to put the butterfly case back above my bedside table. Every day when I open my eyes I say Hello to Orange Albatross and Magpie Crow. I say Goodnight to them as well. But at any time of day, if I touch the case gently and close my eyes, I can see my Gran and Autumn Leaf Gadding About together in the Indian sunshine.

ANN ABINERI

Owen Learning

At first his chick mouth muzzles,
pink hands paw, learning tenderness
at her breast, her milk distils
all he needs for now.

I watch their shared brown eyes
meet and stay, how she doesn't turn away
until he wears
the sated smile, bloated belly
of a little king;

through months of drowsing afternoons or moonlight room
the flowing sweetness fills them both; his vellum skin
rounding out – and for his mother a quiet surprise
at how milk-made love flows both ways.

He knows this place, has known every day
and so has grown a heart of trust;
the cradle of her lap, her offering
of safety in this world;

until, now and then, a cheeky nip;
he turns aside, keen to know
his widening world; she lets him go a little, a little,
as he stands on his own grown ground.

I watch my child
feed her child
and feel full too, and wonder
> how she knows to do that – not from me
> but from the mother we all are.

HELEN CURTIS

Now

Breathless he runs toward his teammates
who call out, 'C'mon, let's play!'
He passes his grandmother
who sits expectantly on a bench
and reaches out from habit
to touch his sleeve.
'Not now,' he scolds.

He sees the hurt on that beloved face.
For a split second, stories, songs and games
embedded in his memories of childhood
make him feel that he should go back,
say something to her,
though he is not sure what.
Instead he rushes on to where he wants to be now.

UTE CARSON

What Will Survive Of Us Is Love

Side by side, we stood in a stone circle, then an opulent hotel, to tell our families and friends of our intention to walk through life together. Love, the abstract concept, underpinned it all; a name for habits we had formed, the tea brewed in a particular cup, the folded down corners of bedsheets, the toothbrushes leaning like silent conspirators; the things that seemed faintly absurd to others, that made total sense to us.

Ordinary existences in family settings rarely invite scrutiny. Our children have filled the spaces we have created for them, and rainbow mountains of laundry now accentuate our rooms with colour. Ideas rich and plentiful, tumble fathoms deep within our home and push at the seams of the fabric of our family life. And so, our love takes shape.

We are busy. There is not enough time, we pass like night bound freighters, blue lights calling us to slump, whale heavy, to beach on the sofa, side by side in front of films and constructed realities. Yet still, our hands connect, yours and mine, together; a sharp shock of tenderness.

When we first held hands, tentatively reaching for each other, I did not know we would sit as we do nearly sixteen years later. Our hands have held us together, ringed with promises, held fast by cords, now coiling close in comfort and habit. We exist, we persist against time, as summers rise and the calls of our children, those becoming, throng our ears. Our past recedes and rests in the earth, like the hazel trees we planted, rooting down, enduring.

Being parents, we can feel washed of our former identities and loves, our former selves lifting away like slow skeins of smoke, rising above the embers of our history. We change; the story of our family and the constellations of beings within it pulls the fabric together, so we may be woven anew; yet our attitude remains. As time weaves, and works us into something new, the fabric of a new love comes into being; we still wear each other like familiar garments, renewed, embellished with blazon parts, the spirits of our children going into the world.

So when the baby unshells us from sleep, the small satellites in our home forge out of orbit on their own trajectories, our past recedes and the future rises over the horizon. Photographs crouch in frames, remembering our details, marking latitude in our family map of existence; under spread eagled night skies, there are sharp hints of our onward journeys. Gazing skywards I know time will transfigure us into memories, images, gestures learned, a turn of phrase, our children walking into the halls of tomorrow, where we cannot tread; yet what we had and what we have is their legacy and the warp and weft of their beings; what will survive of us is love.

ALISON JONES

Index
of Writers with Select Biographies

Ann Abineri (p. 68, 86)

Ann Abineri grew up in Colchester where she first tasted writing success with a road safety essay. In her teens Ann wrote for the school magazine and was the youngest member of a very strange poetry society. After moving to Cambridge to train as a nurse, Ann brought up four children, studied with the OU and now teaches in the childcare and education sector. Ann has had success with poetry, flash fiction and short stories in a range of publications including *Mslexia*, Mother's Milk and Words and Women.

Joanne Adams (p. 46)

Joanne Adams lives in the north east of England with her three beautiful children. This poem was written for her middle child, Arlo, inspired by the closeness of sleeping wrapped up together.

Dawn Allen (p. 41)

Dawn Allen is a full-time mother with a passion for writing. She has a keen interest in the role of creativity in expressing and enhancing the joys and challenges of family life. She loves music, reading, and attempting to knit. She lives in Cambridgeshire with her three children aged from toddler to teen.

Lynn Blair (p. 29)

Lynn Blair is a writer, Cultural and Creative Industries lecturer, musician and home educating mother of four. She creates in a purple shed in the corner of her garden and writes the blog Making Clay. Previous works have been published by the Scottish Book Trust, Mothers Milk Books and *JUNO* magazine. On Twitter she's: @makingclayblog

Cathy Bryant (p. 35, 74)
Cathy Bryant worked as a life model, civil servant and childminder before becoming a professional writer. She has won 24 literary awards and her work has appeared in over 250 publications. Cathy has had two poetry collections published: *Contains Strong Language and Scenes of a Sexual Nature* (Puppywolf, 2010) and *Look at All the Women* (Mother's Milk Books, 2014). See Cathy's listings for cash-strapped writers at: www.compsandcalls.com

Ute Carson (p. 92)
A writer from youth, German-born Ute Carson has published three novels, three collections of poetry and numerous essays and short stories. She resides in Austin, Texas with her husband. They have three daughters, six grandchildren, a horse and a number of cats. Please visit her website: www.utecarson.com

Lanora Clarke (p. 57)

Caroline Cole (p. 62)
I home educate my two children, Ewan, aged six, and Tessa, aged three. I also work part-time as a Forest School Practitioner and write for natural parenting magazines and occasionally on my blog: stoneageparenting.com. We love going on outdoor family adventures in the local woods, hills and moors, as well as further afield travelling abroad together.

Helen Curtis (p. 90)

Helen Curtis (pen-name Robyn Curtis) lives in Derbyshire, near to some of her family, including a little grandson who helps her see things as new all over again. Retired from teaching, she now has the luxury of time and space. She writes poetry and dabbles with art, getting most of her inspiration from wandering in the open on foot or by bike with many stops in cafes for essential note-making.

Jan Dean (p. 27)

Jan Dean is from the North West and lives in the South West. She works as a poet-in-schools.

Alex Habeeb (p. 54)

Karen Harvey (p. 44)

Karen Harvey, Poet and Writing for Wellbeing Facilitator lives on the beach in North Wales with her husband of 41 years, and their granddaughter. Her poem celebrates the water birth of their 6th child Rebecca, and their special relationship with the sea. Karen is keen to support Mothers Milk Books as she nursed all six of her children.

Maeve Henry (p. 67)

Maeve Henry lives in Oxford. She works in hospital administration and is currently studying for a Masters in Creative Writing at Oxford Brookes. Her work has been published in various places, including *Mslexia, The Interpreter's House* and *Ink, Sweat and Tears*. She was longlisted for the National Poetry Competition 2014 and 2015. She is married and has three children.

Angi Holden (p. 84)

Angi Holden is a freelance writer, whose work includes prize-winning adult and children's poetry, short stories and flash fictions, published in online and print anthologies. She brings a wide range of personal experience to her writing, alongside a passion for lifelong learning, Her family are central to her life and her research into family history is a significant influence on her work. She was the winner of the inaugural Mother's Milk Books Pamphlet Prize and her pamphlet, *Spools of Thread* will be published by Mother's Milk Books in 2017.

Tracey Holland (p. 75)

T.D. Holland lives in Nottingham. Tracey is currently studying an MA in creative writing at NTU and is very active in the popular Nottingham literary scene. She has had numerous short stories published but is now working towards finishing her first book, a memoir, which you can a read an excerpt from in this anthology.

Charvi Jain (p. 55)

Alison Jones (p. 93)

Alison Jones lives in Oxford with her three children and husband. She is an English and Media Studies teacher, as well as a writer and poet.

Karen Little (78)

Karen Little trained as a dancer at London Contemporary Dance School, and as a Fine Artist at Camberwell School of Art, London. She has performed and exhibited internationally. Her poems have been published in over fifty magazines and anthologies. *Filled with Ghosts* was published in December 2015, and was shortlisted for the novella Saboteur Award in

2016. *Tentacles: ten Poems, ten Illustrations*, was published in June 2016.

Carmina Masoliver (p. 85)
Carmina Masoliver is a poet, performer and teacher. She is founder of She Grrrowls art events, writer for *The Norwich Radical*, and has had a small collection published by Nasty Little Press. She has shared her poetry at festivals such as Latitude, and in publications such as *Popshot*. She currently lives and works in Spain.

Tiffany 'TJ' McReynolds (p. 56)

Beth McDonough (p. 28)
Beth McDonough trained in Silversmithing at GSA, completing her M.Litt at Dundee University. Writer in Residence at Dundee Contemporary Arts 2014—16, her poetry appears in *Gutter*, *The Interpreter's House* and *Antiphon* and elsewhere. She reviews for *DURA*. *Handfast*, her pamphlet with Ruth Aylett, (Mother's Milk Books, 2016) charts family experiences – Aylett's of dementia and McDonough's of autism.

Rachel Newman (p. 80)
I am an optometrist but now spend my time writing and renovating our farmhouse with my husband Chris, a vet. I write articles and fiction and have just finished a novel set in the veterinary world. Currently, I am working on a memoir and a novel, both inspired by our vineyard, planted on the redundant paddocks when our daughters and their horses left home.

Dawn Osabwa (p. 36)
Dawn Osabwa is a soul-writer, birth-alchemist and a

transformational life coach to those who find themselves lost between realms — who have shed something of the drudgery that has held them back from the magic and sparkle they crave and know to be possible yet for whom the path ahead is not clear. She welcomes them to journey inwards back to their Truth so that they may dance into their lives to the rhythm of their own inner sacred drum. dawn@dancingintolife.com.

Rachel Patel (p. 24)
I live in Cambridgeshire with my husband, daughter and forest cat. Writing and running keep me sane. Having my daughter has helped me to appreciate the world we live in more. We love walking in wellies and seeing what we can see, hear and taste! A good day is when we come home covered with the inky stain of blackberries.

Liz Proctor (p. 47)
Liz lives, works and writes at home in Suffolk, endlessly exploring the fine balance between consultancy, coaching, child-wrangling and creativity. She is trying to make peace with the term home-maker (even though she works almost full time) and secretly wonders whether anyone would pay her to spend her days cycling and playing in the garden. Find her blog at: liveandworkathome.net

I. Rawlinson (p. 53)
My name is Isabella and I am 10. I enjoy playing sports and creative writing.

Ruby Lamey Sarkar (p. 58)

Finola Scott (p. 73)
Finola Scott's poems and stories have won and been placed in

national competitions. She is widely published, in *The Ofi Press*, *The Lake*, *Fat Damsel*, as well as in eight forthcoming anthologies. Liz Lochhead mentors her on the Clydebuilt Scheme. Finola is proud to be a slam-winning granny. She enjoys chocolate, mahjong and her grandgirls, not necessarily in that order.

Catherine Smith (p. 34)
Catherine Smith is a mother of three busy daughters, ages nine, six and two, whom she home educates. She keeps a veritable menagerie of animals and enjoys living green, reading, tramping about the countryside, swimming in the sea and painting.

Deborah Staunton (p. 66)
Deborah L. Staunton's work has appeared in magazines and journals including, *The Sondheim Review*, *Writers' Journal*, *Sheepshead Review*, *Mothers Always Write*, *Meat For Tea* and *The MacGuffin*. She has written child development materials for Harcourt Learning Direct and her essays 'Promises Kept', 'An Owl In Winter', 'Anything Could Happen' and 'Shoes' placed in various writing contests. She lives with her husband Dominic, 11-year-old daughter, Sophie and six-year-old son, Sam on Long Island, New York.

Claire Stephenson (p. 49)
Claire Stephenson is one of the organisers of Fictions of Every Kind, a non-profit literary social event. Her writing was first published in *LS13: A New Generation of Leeds Writers* and more recently in two anthologies by Fair Acre Press, one on spiders and the other on stinging nettles. She loves being in the water, mesostics and goldfinches.

Fern Thomas (p. 69)

Fern Thomas is an artist and mother living in Swansea with her partner and toddler.

Nicky Torode (p. 51)

Nicky Torode is a tutor, career coach, educational resources writer and creative writer. She is a lover of flash fiction, prose poems and vignettes. She believes in the power of the written word to heal. Her Write to Work course uses expressive writing and journalling to help keep up motivation, increase confidence and find your dream job.

Sheila Wild (p. 40)

Sheila Wild was born in Somerset and now lives in the South Pennines. She is a mother, grandmother, policy analyst and poet. Her writing has been described as elegant, beautifully gauged and powerful. Her first collection *Equinox* was published by Cinnamon Press in May 2016.

Sarah Willis (p. 59)

Born in 1989, Sarah Willis is a millennial mother. She is currently attempting to pick apart what this actually means in between working as a Choir Leader, raising her daughter, Indigo, and trying to pull off leopard print. She lives in Hampshire with her hippy boyfriend and her Mum, who is helping her figure this motherhood thing out.

About the Judges

Sarah James (poetry judge)

Sarah James is an award-winning poet, fiction writer and journalist, with six published poetry books, a touring play and a novella out in 2017. Her poems have featured on buses, poetry trails, phone apps, screen savers, poetryfilms, a café mural, at Edinburgh Festival Fringe and in the Blackpool Illuminations. Her collections include: *Lampshades & Glass Rivers* (Loughborough University, 2016), Overton Poetry Prize winner 2015; *plenty-fish* (Nine Arches Press, 2015), shortlisted in International Rubery Book Award 2016; *The Magnetic Diaries* (Knives Forks and Spoons Press, 2015), highly commended in Forward Prize; *Hearth* (Mother's Milk Books, 2015) with Angela Topping; *Be[yond]* (Knives Forks And Spoons Press, 2013) and *Into the Yell* (Circaidy Gregory Press, 2010), third prize in International Rubery Book Award 2011. She also runs V. Press poetry and flash fiction imprint. Website: www.sarah-james.co.uk

Zion Lights (prose judge)

Zion is Contributing Editor of *JUNO* Magazine, author of *The Ultimate Guide to Green Parenting*, and is currently studying for an MSc. She blogs at Science Mum: From the Soil to the Stars: sustainablesciencefamily.blogspot.co.uk and is active on Twitter: @ziontree

Mother's Milk Books
is an independent press, founded and managed by
at-home mother, Dr Teika Bellamy.

The aim of the press is to publish high-quality, beautiful books
that normalize breastfeeding, empower parents, provide
positive role models and encourage creativity.
The annual Mother's Milk Books Writing Prize, which
welcomes poetry and prose from both adults and children,
runs from November to the end of January.
Mother's Milk Books also produces and sells art
and poetry prints, as well as greetings cards.
For more information about the press, and to make purchases
from the online store,
please visit: www.mothersmilkbooks.com